Ponderings

Gail Carpenter

Jan-Carol
Publishing, Inc
"every story needs a book"

Ponderings
Gail Carpenter

Published December 2017
Express Editions
Imprint of Jan-Carol Publishing, Inc
All rights reserved
Copyright © 2017 by Gail Carpenter

This book may not be reproduced in whole or part, in any manner whatsoever without written permission, with the exception of brief quotations within book reviews or articles.

Jan-Carol Publishing, Inc. is committed to publishing works of quality and integrity. In that spirit, we present this book to our readers; however, the stories, the experiences, opinions, thoughts and words are of the author entirely and of the author's recollection. Jan-Carol Publishing, Inc. and the author assume no liabilities of any kind with respect to accuracy of contents or implied.

Every picture in this book was photographed by the author and digitally enhanced by the art consultant.

ISBN: 978-1-945619-50-2
Library of Congress Control Number: 2017962954

You may contact the publisher:
Jan-Carol Publishing, Inc
PO Box 701
Johnson City, TN 37605
publisher@jancarolpublishing.com
jancarolpublishing.com

*This book is dedicated
to my nine grandchildren:
Hannah, Ben, Josh, Gabe, Dave,
Gracie, Noah, Emma, and Faith.*

My thanks to Teresa Wilkerson for her guidance in art,
and to Debbie Robertson for her typing.

Without them, this book would not exist.

We never know what's around the next corner in life.

Dave and Gabe learning to share.

Table of Contents

Life Can	1
Progress	3
The Sustainer	5
Alone	7
A Tribute	9
The Chocolate Cat	11
Remembering My First Granddaughter	17
The Last Goodbye	19
Truths I Have Discovered Along the Way...	21
Talking to God	23
My Religious Beliefs	25
Road Map for Living	27
Family Dynamics	33
Heartbreak and Pain	37
Praise for Rex	41
Life at 518 East Moler Avenue	45
A Meltdown	49
Looking at Religion	51
Adopted by a Cat	55
A Trip to the Cemetery	57

Life Can

Life can whip one to and fro,
Like the last child on the receiving end
In a game of "crack the whip."
Life can hurl the bad at one,
Like bowling balls rolling mercilessly
At unguarded, defenseless pins.
One will traverse refining fire,
Partaking of agony, grief, and despair,
Before earthly life is deemed complete.

This poem was written while my life was completely upside-down. It was the first year after my marital breakup, and we (M and I) lived in a dinky little apartment.

Progress

Each of us,
At some predestined time,
Is going to leave
This world through death.
So why not live in the hope
And anticipation of life
Of a different sort,
After leaving
The world we know.
August 3, 1964

I wrote this poem while at the funeral of my mother's cousin (Dixon-Henry Selma N.C.). I was thinking about how he had wasted his life on alcohol. My first child (M) was born exactly four years later (August 3, 1968).

The Sustainer

Jesus is my life sustainer;
He will tell me where to go;
When I fall, He will remain there...
Pick me up and love me so.

When I find new paths to follow,
And I need his will to know;
On my knees I'll ask his guidance,
Then the pathway He will show.

You must know that He has spoken
To your heart many a time;
When you pray you must turn upward,
With your heart, your soul and mind.

You can tell the hungry people
That there is someone to know,
Who can help with all their sorrow;
He can carry all the load.

Jesus said if you will trust me
I can lead you every day;
It's a promise He has spoken.
Won't you let Him lead the way?

Many people do not know Him;
There are those who have not heard;
While you're here you must be busy
Making sure they hear God's word.

Chorus:
He sustains when we believe Him;
He will guide us when we pray;
Let His presence give us courage
For the living of this day.

Gail wrote words and tune, but Ellen Fulk added proper notes for the tune that God gave Gail. (1995)

Alone

In desolate rain,
At darkest midnight,
The bedraggled soul stood
Waiting for the light and luck to change,
Waiting for life to change,
Waiting for the green light of life.

A Tribute

I know a woman whom God has gifted with special gifts and talents continuing into "old age." At age 97, she can walk around on her own, to attend Sunday School and church regularly, and has mental acuity far greater than most of us in our 70s and 80s. She has wisdom, understanding, and God's grace in relating to others.

She uses the telephone as a ministry, whereby she calls every member possible of her church (360+) on their birthday to wish each one a happy birthday. She can quote several chapters from the Holy Bible. She performs a "Minnie Pearl" skit that would rival the original.

She didn't learn to swim until she was past 80 years of age; then she tackled the diving board with gusto. At age 97, she still takes water aerobics at Reeves Community Center.

And did I mention that she writes poetry that is usually centered on God. I marvel at how God is using her.

Her name is Frances Clifton, and she is an inspiration to all who know her. We can all marvel at how generous God has been to Frances Clifton with long years, sound mind and body, and we can marvel at how she uses her time and telephone to brighten others' day. Her example reminds us that if we fully use whatever talents, skills, and money we have, God will help us make the most of it!

Best wishes to Frances from a Sunday School Classmate!

(January 2002) The following story is about my friend, Mary Lee.

Last night she shared a poignant story about her mother and family. During the past couple of years, her ailing mother has lived in the home of her brother near Dobson, NC. During that two years, Mary Lee has had a hysterectomy and neck surgery from a wreck. Due to years of a strained relationship with the brother, she and her sister did not visit their mother in the brother's home because they realized that she would not know them anyway. However, they had assumed that he would notify them if anything drastic took place.

A few days ago, Mary Lee stumbled on the fact that her mother died over six months ago! The brother had kept it all secret from them. They did not even get to say goodbye to their mother nor participate in her funeral. The brother had made sure that there was no notice in the newspaper, radio, and no write up at the funeral home. The mother had requested to be buried in the ground, but he had her cremated, then put the little box of remains in the ground at an old family cemetery. He did put up a decent stone.

When Mary Lee and Jane began playing detective, they found the funeral home that had been used. They saw the death certificate. Their sister-in-law had signed it. They knew that their mother had sufficient money for a proper burial. They surmised that their brother chose cremation to save the money for his own use.

First, they went to a well-kept cemetery and searched every headstone two times before finally concluding that their mother was not buried there.

When they finally found the correct cemetery, it was almost dark on a very cold January evening. When they found their mother's headstone, her sister Jane (age 62) broke down in tears and threw herself on her mother's grave. They thought their mother was in a casket under the ground.

When they later learned that only her ashes lay buried there, they were even more disconsolate. Within two weeks, they arranged to have their own minister conduct a personal gravesite service just for the two of them to assist in their closure.

Family rifts unresolved can last to the grave.

The Chocolate Cat
(True Story)

Into my life has come a cat who has slowly warmed my heart. I have never liked black cats. I guess it was mainly that old superstition. Anyway, hating to waste anything, I have developed a habit of putting all my food scraps and peelings out in the edge of the yard somewhat under a bush, so that any animal so inclined could partake. (For two or three years I have fed a ground hog who came after dark to check out the daily menu.)

This year I became aware that a black "neighbor cat" was raiding my scrap pile with some regularity. After I spoke kindly to her for several days, she stopped running away and would stay to watch me water my plants, then she would disappear. Eventually, we became acquainted enough that she would let me rub her fur. I became aware that only her head is black; the rest of her is chocolate brown. That makes her special because I have never met another chocolate brown cat. (And I thought with relief, *well, she's not black.*)

The cat seemed desperately thin; it appeared that my random scraps were her only food supply. Since she was still too skittish to have me turn her over and check her out, I decided to name her Samantha which would become "Sam" if "she" was a "he."

By now my excess food leftovers were going directly into a dish at the back door for Samantha, who appeared and disappeared twice a day. I began to have thoughts of having her spayed so she wouldn't end up pregnant and deliver a litter in one of my flower beds, but I didn't want to take someone's cat. I began to walk thru the circle of apartments behind me in search of where she called "home" when she was not visiting me. I never saw her at any of the apartments.

Little by little, I took on the responsibility for seeing to it that Samantha got two square meals a day. I remember standing in the grocery store deciding to buy a box of dry cat food to fill in on days when my scraps were sparse. (I have not owned a cat or cat food for many years.) Inch by inch, this cat was leading me down a path of ownership, which I traveled willingly.

The timing of this event was rather remarkable. I have been allergic to cats (and half the world) for over 15 years. Through use of some special nutrients, my immune system has improved incredibly; so that while taking the nutrients, I can tolerate having an animal around!

Two days later, I had a unique reception committee waiting when I arrived home: sitting in my flower bed was Samantha and her only child, a kitten who appeared to be about three weeks old. I finally figured out what had happened. A family had moved away from the apartments, and left behind one pregnant cat (Samantha). The kitten was well-marked with a handsome gray and white. I suspected it was a boy, but I could not yet touch it. It had been a "street kid" all its young life, and expected the worst from humans. Although dependent upon Mama for nourishment, it was very feisty, and would make a brave effort to defend itself when necessary.

They lived in my flower beds for the next few days while I decided how to handle being owned by a cat and kitten. When the rains came, they moved under the big oil drum until the sun came out. When I came too close, the kitten hid well under the snap dragons.

One day the kitten was sitting right at the back door when I was ready to go in; I told Samantha she had "planted" him there to look so cute. Of course, he was still too skittish to be touched, but that would come in time.

I asked Rex to build a small swinging cat-door at the bottom of my garage door. Well, we all made a deal: Rex and the cat Samantha, and I. Rex would build the door; I would keep the cats in my garage, and Samantha would keep all the mice out of my garage and away from the books and pictures located in said garage.

One of the next steps would be a trip to the vet for spaying. However, I needed advice on when the proper timing for that would be. I planned to call my doctor daughter, who almost became a vet, so she could advise me.

It's funny all the little things God can send to brighten up your life just when you need it...like a chocolate cat with a little gray and white kitten.

Remembering Samantha

Yesterday Rex and I lost our best friend. Her name was Samantha. Retracing the story from Part 1, when her daughter, Lillian was killed by the traffic of Moler Avenue, we decided to move Samantha from the garage into the house.

Little by little, she filled our hearts with joy. All his life, Rex had never been "silly" over cats like some people get. To him, most of them are just animals that must be fed. That's where Samantha differs—why she captured his heart. Her personality came partly from having been on her own, learning how to survive, how to be cautious, how she might better herself. She came here in need of our love, and when she became satisfied that she could trust us, she returned that love. Sam and Rex developed a camaraderie to the extent that seemed to be like a human understanding between the two of them. Rex began to look forward to Sam coming to his truck to greet him upon his arrival. She had a special vocal "hello" to welcome her buddy, Rex. After that she went to "her" tree and did her claw exercise, as if she was excited that Rex had come to see her. Anytime he went past her, she greeted him with that special meow. It was

Ponderings

a satisfying pleasure; wherever we worked in the yard, she would be right there tagging along. She was so pleased to be with us that sometimes she rolled and turned her little belly up as if she wanted us to play with her. But she was such a refined personality that she wanted us to know that she had restraints, so she gently acted as if she were going to fend us off, yet she did not extend her claws.

When she wanted to come into the house, she would often stand on two legs and "knock" on the glass door with her front paws. It sounded much like the knock of a person. She made trips to the upstairs bathroom to get fresh water from a dripping cold faucet. As she jumped down from the sink and came down the stairs, she sounded as noisy as a small child. She reminded us that she was sharing the house. She appreciated our house and yard to the extent that she developed an attitude that everything belonging to us was definitely hers... every inch of the yard also.

When she first moved in, she claimed the big green chair in the living room; later she perched on the back of the white couch. Occasionally, she tested me to ask if she could share my bed, but I had to tell her "no" by moving her over to a chair in my bedroom. Often, she would lie and watch me till I went to sleep. She developed a little ritual of never going back downstairs to the kitchen until I was up to accompany her. We went down the stairs together, and I dipped a little dry food into her good dish and gently rubbed her back a couple of times, after which she began to eat and sing at the same time!

She was truly beautiful with her soft black fur and large green eyes filled with love as if she adored us.

She could pull open the louvered doors toward the front porch. Sometimes she chose to sit in the big box I have out there. Her favorite toy was a little sock filled with catnip. I offered her store-bought toys, but she generally ignored them favoring either the catnip or playing with Rex and a piece of string.

She developed definite taste regarding foods. Even though she started with the compost pile, once inside she decided not to eat most table scraps. However, she liked the smell of sliced roast beef. In canned cat food, her favorite was the Alpo tuna. She did not care for milk.

Every day when I left for work she and I said goodbye, and every day when I returned, she was right there to say hello. In many ways, she was more like a dog because she followed me (or us) around outside. If I planted a flower, she was there to supervise. I realize that most cats can learn a certain amount of our vocabulary, but she seemed to be so highly intelligent that I just pretended that she understood everything I said, and she either understood or pretended to!

She loved to be outside during the night, so when the temperature was not too drastic, we would let her make the decision of inside or outside. We still had the light bulb set up in the garage to take off the chill on the questionable weather.

Sam didn't chase birds, and she didn't cow tail to dogs. When I worked at the computer, she often asked to be held. I was hesitant to hold her because of my allergies, but she knew how to persuade me. At the table, she asked to sample the food. Rex would rearrange the chairs rather than scoot her off a chair.

Rex and I noticed a growth on the side of her body which seemed to be getting larger. We took her to the veterinarian who scheduled surgery for the next day. I held her when she was on the examining table; before we left her there, she kissed me! When we brought her back home, her head was drooping and she was still groggy. Her side looked gross with the hair all shaved off and the large stitches. A couple of days after the stitches were removed, she began begging to go outside. I knew that she was somewhat weak, but I gave in and opened the back door for her. My thoughts were that she could go into the garage if needed, and she could always climb a tree if a dog gets too close.

The next morning, she did not come to the door as usual. I called Rex; he came over and found her dead in the middle of the back yard. I had forgotten that the groundhog who lived under a tool shed at the far back of the yard might be a threat for her. I felt very guilty for not using better judgment and keeping her inside until she was completely recovered. Often in life we wish we could relive (and change) a moment; I wished that I could change my decision to allow Sam outside.

Rex made a coffin for Sam out of the finest walnut wood in his workshop, and he buried her in my flower beds at the very back of the yard. When Samantha lost her life, we were losers too. She made our world a much nicer place!

Remembering My First Granddaughter

(Below are a few special moments that we shared)

In September, you directed me to sit in the rocking chair in your room (at your house) because, "Grandmas are supposed to sit in rocking chairs."

During one of my bad coughing spasms, you were patting me on the back hip (it was as high as you could reach on my back) and saying, "bless you" over and over. It was so dear!

At one of our nap times (at my house), you were singing a song about wishing daddy could come down from the sky. (My heart cried for you.)

On two occasions in November, you spoke (at bedtime) of heaven and your Dad. You said that you were going to heaven; you asked if his hair will be long.

After some phone interruption of my monologue, I came back and said "Now, where were we?" H replied, "You were in the rocking chair, and I was in bed." The literal way children think is so precious!

You have recently preceded your sentences with the following phrases: "I'll tell you what...;" "Let me tell you...;" and "I was wondering..." When I asked

Ponderings

where you had heard the phrase, "I was wondering," you replied, "From the movie *Shrek*." You soak up everything just like a little sponge.

You stayed with me from November 28 to December 2, 2001. We had a very full agenda during your visit. You went with me to choir practice and behaved quite well for a 3-year-old, but you told me much later that it hurt your ears! Truthfully, she does play the piano too loud for such a small room. We baked little cakes, sent G a card, saw the video *Charlotte's Web* as an early present, took poinsettias to the daycare personnel, went to movie *102 Dalmatians*, went to my Sunday School class, and to play at McDonald's—a full four days!

Lately, you told me to "get control of myself." I tried not to laugh. I assumed that this was a new phrase that your Mom used with you.

Since your Mom took over care of your haircuts, your hair had been growing longer. Your hair was still blond, but with the hint of dark underneath. Your Mom was getting very good at taking pictures and recently made some special ones of you at the Christmas tree.

When Uncle J held you and tickled you, you seemed to respond with great enthusiasm. He also bounced you, pretending that his body was a boat traveling over the waves, and you loved it!

When you were with me, you loved to play pretend games. Sometimes you were the doctor with me as the patient; you usually "operated" on my foot; sometimes you dressed up all in red as "Little Red Riding Hood," sometimes you dressed up as Mary Poppins, and sometimes Dorothy from *Wizard of Oz*. One day after we returned home from church, you insisted on wearing the outfit that I had on, so I had you stand on an ottoman so I could make your picture in my dress. It turned out great!

When you were here at my house, you often wanted to do exactly what I did. Therefore, when I placed a glass of water and cough drop at my bedside table, you insisted on also having a glass of water and cough drop ready for you.

You were still getting an afternoon nap most days, however, there were days when activities made that impossible. On nap days, you did not get to bed until 9:30 or 10:00 pm. You were going to potty by yourself.

You were very advanced in terms of vocabulary and auditory learning; however, you seldom sat still very long for me to read to you. You preferred to pretend to read yourself. You were not greatly interested in learning numbers beyond ten or practicing the alphabet yet; hopefully this would soon change.

When you turned four years old in February, I knew your party would be held at McDonald's. After you got a little older, Mom would probably have the parties at your house. For a home party, you-all needed to be old enough to sit down and play games together.

The Last Goodbye

What to say when, instinctively, you know it's a last goodbye? I have packed the car, and I am almost ready to drive across three states. He sits relaxed on the old unpainted boards of the side porch of a quiet country house where he was born some 75 years back down the road of life. As his legs hang off the porch's edge, his feet shift the dirt on the ground in a slow thoughtless pattern.

His shifting feet tell me that he has something weighing on his mind. I broach the subject for him. I assure him that, as his loving niece, I support him in his need of friendship with a lady his own age; although no one could replace the memory of his deceased wife. I see gratitude in his face with no words spoken. I assure him that, with a little time, his daughter will think in a like manner. I have answered a question that he had been too hesitant to ask, and I see the relief in his eyes.

As I hug him and gently kiss his weathered cheek, I know inside that this is a final goodbye...a parting. The eyes...they tell me that he knows it too. As we speak the parting words, neither of us chooses to acknowledge the tears we are sharing... Farewell, dear gentle soul.

I wrote this article about my mother's brother. The incident happened as described. I wrote it about September 1982.

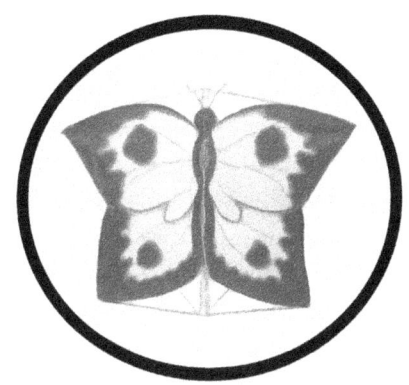

Truths I Have Discovered Along the Way

"Into each life some rain must fall." Everyone—no matter how rich or poor, how educated or uneducated—will have trials, tribulations, headaches, and heartaches. But, the main difference is that the Christian can lean on God during those times (lean one's head on our Father's shoulder for Comfort.)

"Judge not that you be not judged." When you observe a person's behavior, lifestyle, or sin, remember that you are seeing that person only as he is at the present time. Remember that he may not have been like that in the past, and that he may not be like that in the future. We must learn that people keep changing, just like things and circumstances keep changing. Sometimes when another person observes a "backslidden" Christian, the observer thinks of him as a hypocrite or as insincere from that time forth. We must remember that all of us are fallible human beings and that only Jesus was/is perfect, and that by keeping our eyes on Christ, we will "fall" less often.

"Turn your eyes upon Jesus. Only Jesus will not forsake you." When we become too dependent upon another human being, we are headed for disappointments. I keep having to learn this over and over again. Did you ever feel that your friend has let you down? Or your husband? Your wife? Your parent? That is sure to happen because all of us humans are fallible and we will (either intentionally, willfully, or unintentionally, unwillfully) disappoint others who depend upon us. We must place ourselves in the hands of God—literally depend on God more than on our spouses, our children, or our friends.

We adults should not advise a child or another adult to pray about a particular thing. We should stop and pray aloud with the person who asked for our help. I remember once I consulted my grandmother about a matter very important to my life at that time. She told me to pray about it, and that ended the conversation. Good advice, but often not sufficient. I did not know how to really talk to God (pray) at that time in my life. How extremely significant in my life it would have been if she had stopped then and there and prayed aloud with me about the matter! I know that she had read through her bible three times before she died; but, at that moment, she missed her opportunity to help someone find his/her way into a closer relationship with her God! Pray with the person who expresses a need!

Talking to God

  I have come to firmly believe that God expects us to "connect" with Him every day. It could be compared to getting our "battery charged" daily in preparation for the following day. Just as the electric cars must stop for "recharging," so do we, and things work better if we "recharge" on a daily basis as God has intended.

  In our daily visit with God, we should mention everything for which we are thankful during the past 24 hours, especially the little things. (When we learn to consistently pay attention to the little things in life, we will have grown spiritually.) In this thankful attitude, we should praise Him saying, "Blessings, Honor, Glory to your Holy Name" or just saying from the heart, "I Love you Lord."

  We should tell Him exactly how we feel about the things that are on our mind/heart. Talk it over with Him. There is no reason to hold anything back. God knows everything we've ever said or done. He sees clear through us and "reads" our hearts.

  We should ask His forgiveness and for guidance for ourselves, and for those who are on our personal prayer list.

  We should request wisdom, insight, knowledge, understanding, patience, and faith sufficient for our needs for the next 24 hours.

We should ask God to let us do something for Him (use us in His service) on the following day even if it is in a very small way. (Perhaps even a smile or kind word to someone.)

We should ask him to help us to seek after righteousness.

Setting aside a certain time each day to get our "battery charged" from God will establish it as a habit, and we will thereby be more consistent. For me that time is just before retiring to bed. Included also daily should be some reading from the Bible—perhaps a chapter a day. I suggest reading straight through a book of the Bible rather than randomly opening and reading night after night. One more important thing: before each night reading, ask God to reveal to you the real meaning of the words you are about to read. Ask Him to give you understanding of what you are about to read. I love you....God loves you!

It is a good idea to ask God to let your guardian angels watch over you while you are sleeping.

I do not always follow up on all of these items, but it's what I strive toward. Due to being tired or hurried, I sometimes include only some of them, but I try to include as many as possible.

My Religious Beliefs

When I lived alone in Martinsburg, WV, the Rosedale Cemetery contacted me to say I was chosen to receive a free plot in their cemetery. I accepted it and paid the $60 maintenance fee. They showed me the exact location; I would be placed nearby a planned statue or enclosure on a hillside. I remember reflecting that it was a good location because the rain water would drain on away from the little hill. I'm not sure why that mattered.

The shortest route to my workplace (IRS-MCC) took me right by the cemetery where I could spot that little hill every day. It was certainly a sobering ride in the mornings.

When the Rosedale staff called me from time to time urging me to go ahead and buy the coffin, stone, etc., I would tell them that there is a family cemetery near Selma, NC where I may be buried because I have family buried there.

When I made the decision to move from WV to NC to be closer to both my children, I gave back the free plot to the Rosedale staff. In a discussion with my daughter, M, she suggested that I make my own decisions and arrangements regarding final wishes/funeral. My son agreed that it was a good idea. At first, I was hurt and feeling sorry for myself, but I got past that, and it forced me to not only make decisions about a final resting place, but I have become more organized in doing things that had been left undone for years.

Although I hope to live for years to come, I have been "packing my suitcase" or "tying up loose ends" in many respects and that feels good. I created a special notebook in which I am including funeral information, insurance policies, bank account, and driver's license; all easily accessible.

I recently observed the behavior of a woman who knew for months that she was dying with cancer. She continued to play her card game of bridge and to keep her weekly hair appointment right down to the week before she died. I found it incredible that she could not find other more important things to do with her limited time left here on earth! Had she no desire to leave letters to grandchildren? To complete projects unfinished? To ask somebody's forgiveness? To leave something behind more permanent than an empty chair at the bridge table?

I believe that once inside heaven, God will judge our lifetime behavior and will station us close to Himself (the source of Light and Love) or farther away based on how we handled our life. In other words, our proximity to Him for Eternity within heaven will be just and understood. I believe that my sin of adultery, although forgiven, got me placed further away from God than I would have been if I had not yielded to temptation.

I believe that there is a hell occupied by those who had opportunities and refused to accept Christ as God's way into eternal heaven. Part of that hell will be living without any light or love. Regarding those who have never had an opportunity or chance to hear about God's plan of salvation, I do not have an answer. I guess we'll find out that answer after we die, as with many other things that do not get answered while we occupy a spot here on planet earth.

My view of death and eternity has changed a little over the years, but not very much. I believe that the key to eternity with God is the belief that he paved a way by sending Christ to die on the cross. That belief is our ticket into heaven. If our original ancestors had not yielded to temptation and sinned, we humans would not be struggling with sin on a daily basis, and trying to find our way to Christ.

Road Map for Living

The following information is of a personal and crucial nature. It is written with "hindsight" and, hopefully, acquired wisdom. It is written by one who has sinned big time, asked with a sincere and repentant heart for God's forgiveness, and received it.

Life offers us a "smorgasbord" of things to do, things to see, things to eat. Some of these things are "forbidden fruit" and can harm us one way or another. There are only two ways to know which things in life's "smorgasbord" are off-limits. One is by stumbling into them and receiving the resultant burning, hurting which may last a lifetime. The other (and better) way is by reading the rule book, the Bible, to see what should and should not be tasted.

One eventually learns that over-indulgence in food or drink is abusing one's own body, and that getting no exercise is abusing one's own body. Care for the mind is less obvious. Exposure to pornography via films, magazines, telephone, or personal viewing are all abuse of one's mind. Those who offer us drugs and pornography have a greed for money.

Many people choose to ignore the following: God is real! Jesus is real! Satan is real! Demon helpers of Satan are real! Angels are real! Let's see how it all fits together.

Sometimes we open a "door" (even just a crack in the door is sufficient) so that Satan's demons may enter our body/mind or homes and play havoc. This "opportunity" may come through use of a Ouija board, going to a fortune teller, playing mind games, or some obvious sin such as adultery. Often the person doesn't even realize he is exposing himself and setting up such an "opportunity."

Many things can happen while one is not walking under God's protection. Strange, unexplainable things can be observed in the home such as radios, TVs turned on or off without human effort, a picture moved on the wall, an object thrown across the room by an "invisible" spirit. The individual may even feel a "punch" or smack from an invisible hand.

What can be done?

Such things should send us fleeing back to God for protection. GOD IS OUR ONLY SOURCE OF PROTECTION.

How does one do that?

One starts by teaching himself to pray. Praying is just talking to God, saying whatever is in your heart. (He already "reads" our hearts anyway, so nothing is secret from Him.) But He expects us to <u>communicate</u> with Him <u>every day,</u> at least once per day. It should become a life-time habit.

The only sense of true peace comes through and from God. (Peace in your heart and peace in your house.) If there is harmony within one's body and spirit, it will be reflected throughout one's house. If there is dis-harmony, that can also be reflected through the house.

Pray daily at bed time. Get down on your knees as a sign of reverence. (A pillow protects your knees.) Every day, as part of your prayers, find some things to thank God for that day (no matter how small). Have a regular "mental list" of people for whom you wish to pray daily. You can ask God to bless those people. Add or subtract people on your list as circumstances dictate.

For yourself and those closest to you, ask God to let your guardian angel watch over you and protect you while you sleep. Ask God to help you to resist temptation while awake and asleep. Ask God to grant to you and your closest people wisdom, insight, knowledge, understanding, faith, hope, and love.

After prayers, read a chapter in your Bible before going to sleep (Before reading, ask God to give you the <u>understanding</u> of what you are about to read). As you read your Bible have a pen and a marker. Use them as you read anything that seems highly significant to you. Make notes in the margins. (After all, it's your own Bible). Start to memorize a special verse or two that has a special meaning for you.

I am thoroughly convinced of one thing...God expects us to communicate with Him on a daily basis, to ask for protection from Satan's helpers and anything else that may harm us. Just as the sun rises every 24 hours, so are we to look to God every 24 hours and more often as one grows spiritually. God made the sun and moon, and He made you and me.

After you have accepted God/Jesus into your heart, there are scriptures that can be especially helpful. When encountering the unknown, you can use the scripture that says, "He that is within me (God) is greater than he that is in the world (Satan) (from 1 John 4:4)." You can say, "I plead that blood of Jesus over me." There is power in the blood of Jesus. You are not stronger than the devil, but God is; so one must ask God to protect him and believe it, and He will. It's the believing that is the key. It brings you on your knees before the Lord of Hosts!

Note: Underlined in my Bible are many verses which have a special meaning for me. I have taken the time to go through the Bible and make note of many of those verses with a brief subject and scripture references where these may be found. These may be helpful as you begin your own search of the scriptures for those verses which "speak" to you personally.

Topical Scriptures

Adam: 1 Cor 15:22
Bible scripture is inspired by God: 2 Tim 3:16
Understanding the scriptures: Luke 24:45
Life's purpose: Colossians 3:1-8, 14-17; 2 John 5:6-12
God's gift: Rom 3:22-25; Rom 5:19
The blood of Jesus: (We can plead the blood of Jesus for protection.)
His blood cleanses us from sin: 1 John 1:7
His blood to purify conscience: Hebrews 9:14
Justified by His blood: Rom 5:9
Peace by blood of cross: Colossians 1:20
Lord guard you from evil: 2 Thes 3:3
God all powerful protector: Rom 8:38
He forgives our sins: Ps 65:2-3; Ps 103:3; Acts 10:43; 1 John 1:12
God judges us all: Ps 96:13; Rom 2:16; Rom 14:11-12; 2 Peter 3:14
Duty of man: Eccl 12:13-14; Isaiah 55:6-9; Rom 2:4-7; Rom 12: 9-13; 1 Tim 4:8-10; 2 Tim 2:22; Titus 2:11-14
Your faith is the key: Matt 9:29; Matt 17:18-20; Matt 18:19-20; Eph 2:8; 1 Peter 1: 6-9; James 1: 5-6; Hebrews 12: 1-2; Rom 14:22; John 6:47; Acts 3:12; Rom 3: 22-25; Rom 5: 1-2; Hebrews 11: 1-3; Hebrews 11:6

Ponderings

God is sovereign: Isaiah 40:22; Isaiah 64:8; Acts 14:15; Rom 1:20; Rev 5:13-14
Angels: Matt 4:11; Matt 13:49; Matt 25:31; Matt 26:53; Matt 28:2; Mark 1:13; Hebrews 13:2; Peter 3:22; Rev 22:16; John 1:51; Acts 27:23; Ps 34:7
God/forever: Ps 73:26; Ps 103:15-18; 2 Cor 5:1; 2 Phil 2:10-11
Prayer to God: Ps 86:11-12; 2 Phil 4:6-7; 2 Phil 4:8-9
God answers prayer in His timing: Ps 69:13; Eph. 3:20
Trust & patience in the Lord: Ps 37: 3-8; Prov. 3:5-6
Pray for each other: James 5:16
Private prayer: Matt 6:6
Duty to pray: Jeremiah 29: 12-13; Luke 18:1
Anchor of the soul: Hebrew 6: 19
Lord's prayer: Matt 6: 9-13
Seek kingdom/righteousness: Matt 6: 33
Christ died for us: 1 Peter 2: 24; 1 John 4: 9-12
Lord in unapproachable light: 1 Tim 6:16
God is our hope/help: Ps 33: 20-22; Rom 10: 9
From fear to trust: Ps 56:3; Ps 62: 8; Matt 10: 31-32; Matt 12: 28-30
Clean heart/new spirit: Ps 51:10-12,17; Proverbs 20:27; John 6:63; Rom 12: 1-2
Spirit from God: 1 Cor 2: 10-13; 1 Cor 3:16; 2 Cor 4:16-18; Eph. 1:13-14; Eph. 2:22
The Holy Spirit: Acts 15:8; 2 Cor 3:18; 2 Tim 1:14
Praying in the spirit: Rom 8: 26-27; Jude 1:20
Worship in spirit: John 4:23-24
Spirit vs. flesh: Galatians 5:16; Eph. 2:3
Fruit of the spirit: Galatians 5: 22-23
Gifts of the spirit: 1 Cor 12: 4-11
Resist temptations: 2 Peter 5: 8-11; Rev 2:10; 1 Thes 5: 21-22; James 1: 12-15
God is greater than Satan: 1 John 4:4; James 4:5-8
Shun Satan: Matt 10:28; 2 Cor 4:4; Eph 6: 12-14
God cares: 2 Peter 5: 7
Love chapter of Bible: 1 Cor 13
God sees and hears: 1 Peter 3:12; 2 John 5:14; Ps 11:4; Ps 33:13-15; Prov 15:3; 1 Cor 4:5
Songs/praise: Ps 69:30; Ps 100:2; Ps 104:33; Ps 118:14
Fear God/depart evil: Job 28:28; Ps 147:11; Isaiah 41:10
God tries minds/hearts: Ps 34:18

Giving: 2 Cor 9: 8-11; Eph 6:8; Hebrews 13:16
God near the broken-hearted: Ps 34:18
Heart/treasure: Luke 12:34
Do not love things of this world: 1 John 2:15
Breath & life is from God: Job 34: 14-15; Eccl 8:8
Save others: Jude 1:22
Faith & forgiving others: Mark 11: 22-25
Suffering for righteousness merits blessings: 1 Peter 3:14; 1 Peter 4:14
Growth as Christians: Hebrews 5:13-14; Peter 2:2-3
We shed this body: 2 Peter 1:14
Unclean spirits: Matt 10:1
Days are numbered: Ps 90:12; Matt 6: 27; Luke 12: 25-26
Love of money: Hebrews 13:5; Eccl: 5:10; Matt 17:26
Spirit into the womb: Eccl 11:5
Widows & orphans: James 1:27
Our mouth/tongue: Matt 12:36; Matt 15:11; Eph 4:29; Col 3:8; James 3:5-12
Conscience: 1 Peter 3:16; 1 Tim 1:5; 2 Col 4:2
Born anew: John 3:3, 14-15
Trials: Acts 14:22
Sewing and reaping: Gal 6:7-10
Burned magic books: Acts 19:19
Homosexual error: Rom 1:24-27; Rom 6:12-13
Mismated: 2 Cor 6:14
Passion of flesh: 1 Peter 2:11
Truth: Ps 51:6
Christ coming: Luke 12:40

How to walk not alone through the world?

Some may view it as too simplistic; others as too complex. It is neither. It is a daily commitment of time with God, which gives you needed protection and a sense of peace unattainable any other way. Even millionaires can't get it any other way!

This may all be done in private. One does not have to "parade" their religion. However, as you accept this commitment, some little things will slowly, gradually change.

For example, formerly, when in an exasperating situation or in a life-threatening situation, one may find himself inadvertently saying a cuss word or the s— word. As you make this daily commitment to communicate with your maker and Lord and Savior, under those same circumstances described above, you will find yourself instead calling on the name of the Lord for help.

Upon arising each morning, ask the Holy Spirit to indwell you and to <u>cast out anything impure from your body, mind, and spirit</u>. DO THIS DAILY.

Prayer and Bible reading will take from 15 to 30 minutes of your time each day. Think you don't have time? Remember that the next day you live and the next breath you take is with God's permission! (Eccl 8:8) (Of course, if you sometimes must omit Bible reading and make an abbreviated prayer, surely God will understand, but it is establishing the daily <u>habit</u> of communicating with God that is so important.)

God gives us each a conscience to act as a rudder or guide to steer us away from things that may harm us such as "forbidden fruit." The more we saturate ourselves with forbidden fruit, such as pornographic material, the less able we are to "hear" the conscience until eventually one may seem to have no conscience at all because he has become so desensitized.

What is life all about anyway?

It is finding our way to acknowledge God, to worship God, to love God, and to seek His will for our lives. After our ancestors (Adam and Eve) messed up a paradise by disobeying God (original sin), He devised a plan and sent His Son to die on a cross to cover humanities' sins. So those who <u>believe</u> He did that can move (after this life on Earth) to an unending existence of paradise beyond our mental capacity to fathom. (Romans 3: 22-25)

Family Dynamics

I wanted to share something with you. When S (L's wife) came over a couple of weeks ago and brought pictures, etc., we talked for a couple of hours, and it was a good talk. She is a nice lady and I actually like her!

She had trouble coping with some of the same things that I did, (temper, unfinished projects, etc.) and the fact that he would not settle with me and move forward. So, after they were married six years, she left him and wanted a divorce. They were separated for one year, during which time he did some changing. They were back together almost three years before he died, and she said those years were happier.

I asked her <u>why</u> she thought he never mailed the letter he had written to you. She said it was because he was afraid…that he didn't know how you felt about him, and that he felt he could not bear it if you rejected him. It seems that he had never told her that he ousted us from the house in a temper tantrum. She thought we just left.

She said he always came home sharing information with her about you any time that he learned any tidbit about you, where you were, what you were doing, accomplishments, etc.

Since I knew she had heard his side of the story many times, I shared a little of my side. I told her that I eventually could no longer cope with the nasty temper and all the unfinished projects surrounding me, and that I knew that he would remind me for the rest of my life of my one infidelity...and that those are the reasons I filed for divorce. (She agreed that he would have.)

What S said next nearly made me fall off my chair. She said, "Gail, quit beating yourself up over the past, because he <u>was no angel</u>! She said that L had told her that he had various secret affairs throughout his marriage to me! The irony is that he threatened to have affairs and to leave me numerous times over the years—and all the time he was actually taking mistresses as he chose to! Those years he worked his second job to buy all that shop equipment were not all work, I presume.

I asked S how long was the longest affair. She said it was for three years! (She does not remember any names since she did not know the people.) She says she told him that he was a hypocrite. She says he felt he didn't really do wrong because he thoroughly believed in the double standard. She says that in his own warped way he actually loved me and the kids.

For days after my talk with S, I went through a whole range of emotions. I started wanting to put names and faces to the infidelities (which is likely impossible now). I remember that during the marriage, I used to feel jealously or lack of security, which I could not understand; now I understand that my instincts were right on target!

S said he was a very complex man. She also said that before he died, he finally learned the difference between love and sex.

She said whenever you reach a point that you are ready and would like to talk to her about your dad, she is open to talking to you either in person at Shepherdstown, or anyplace, or via phone. She seemed to want to be helpful. I wish he had mailed that letter to you ten years ago so that perhaps you two could have been part of each other's lives for the past few years.

Of course, I feel betrayed by him, especially in view of how he harassed me so over my one indiscretion, but I would still have wished you to have a relationship with your father. I just didn't know how to fix the break between you.

I am coming to a realization: It is no wonder that I have developed a chronic illness such as CFIDS. L "beat me up" emotionally both during the long marriage and especially for years after the divorce as he fought to keep me from settling the property. J was spoon-fed propaganda by L presenting me as an adulteress for so long that I think J often thought of me as less than his father... perhaps a bit second class. And you, M, were verbally disrespectful to me for many years for your own reasons. I always thought it was because you lost your father in the process of standing by me when I made the decision to go with the divorce. And I accepted the emotional beating that I received from all of you, and carried my own feelings of guilt for having disrupted everyone's lives. And now I wonder how he dared to be so vindictive toward me when he had been unfaithful to me and the marriage for 19 years.

God has been my source of strength through these last several years. Without him, I just would not have made it. I am grateful to S for sharing with me about L's double life and double standards. I think it freed me of the guilt I still carried.

Family

I am taking some avenues now to work toward getting my health back on track (or at least improved). I am living with a bit of hope again. Many things have taken a toll on my body over the last 15 years. They include M's suicide, our homelessness, divorce, major surgery, burn-out at social work, L's ten years of hostility (toward me) and the never-ending legal battles, mother's death, empty nest syndrome, and numerous car wrecks. After all the stresses over an extended period of time, my body systems could no longer cope. With the grudge, you and your father both held against me, my morale, my ego, my immune system all "took a beating."

YOU can help me get into better health. You hold one key. The long-term negativity and hostility that you send forth toward me affects my mood and my immune system. If you will tell me what you are holding against me, I can address it, and we can try to get past your hostility. About a year ago, you did verbalize two things from your childhood (at age 5 and 11). Neither was directly my fault, but I have asked for your forgiveness.

There must be something more that you have not yet shared with me. Your cussing, drinking, and pushing your body to the edge (such as biking down a mountain at night) are indicators that you are holding in <u>something</u> (in my opinion).

I know that when you encouraged me to go through with the divorce years ago, you assumed that J would live with us. I have already explained <u>why</u> I did not push for that (even though it broke my heart). Could that be part of your hostility?

I do realize that during your teen years (and beyond) I mostly let you be the "boss." That was due to several things:
- I hated confrontations.
- I felt too guilty (from my affair) to stand up for myself.
- You have a dominant personality.

I am gradually letting go of the emotional overload I've been carrying around, but I need your help! I can no longer deal with your disrespect, ridicule, and sharp barbs. I would like to eventually be an integrated part of your life—enjoy any children you may bear or adopt. But it requires change in your attitude toward me.

I have poured out my heart to you in many long letters in the past to which you never responded. This is not just <u>another</u> one of those letters. If you refuse to help me (and yourself), I'll have to go forth without you. I hope you will choose to answer this letter. Do not substitute the telephone for a letter; you can think faster than I can, and our conversations tend to go astray and deteriorate on the phone. I love you.

Heartbreak and Pain

How sad this day of 8/29/95 has been for me. Last night a piece of my heart broke off when my daughter, M, told me I can no longer be part of her life. After what should have been considered a minor disagreement, she said, "Fuck you! You can go to hell, I don't need you! I hate you! You'll never see me again except at my funeral and maybe if you sneak in at my wedding." Then she slammed down the phone.

I guess her resentment has been building up over the past twelve years since our family split at the time of my divorce. When she told me she hated me during her teen years, I figured it was all part of growing up, so I just kept telling her, "I love you." Now that she has gone back to saying, "I hate you" at age 27, I am devastated.

A piece of my heart also broke off in 1983 when I made the decision to encourage my son, J, to choose his father for custody rather than choosing me. Knowing I would not be with J on a daily basis broke my heart, but I made the decision I felt I had to made under the circumstances. (L had threatened suicide if I gained both children and the house; the counselor, Rev. W, suggested that I raise M while L raise J).

A piece of my heart broke off the summer that I went to Annapolis (at J's official invitation) for the end of plebe summer, and sat alone in Dahlgren Hall waiting all day and into the evening until they locked the doors, waiting for J. I was told by the registration desk that J's "mother" had already signed in, and I learned from the card that S had signed as his real mother. I spent the night in an officer's home, and shared a bed with a total stranger (a black woman in similar plight), in order to hope to find our sons in the morning.

Going to the dormitories and seeing J momentarily before he went to a designated spot to once again meet his father and S, and then go on to participate in the program. My heart sank right down into my shoes. I tried in vain to save the tears until I was alone.

I have to wonder how many pieces of the heart one can lose and still have it intact enough to keep the body going? In a poem I read years ago, someone died of a broken heart. Back then, I didn't understand how that could be possible. My, what the ensuing years teach us.

I have had other painful moments in my life which I shall briefly relate, but none of them, including death of family members, broke my heart in the way that losing time and intimacy with my children has done. Luckily, J and I were able to rebuild a relationship through our mutual Christian beliefs. It is my hope and prayer that M and I can rebuild a relationship eventually.

Painful was the fact that at age ten, I was without a father permanently, and without a mother except on weekends for several years. Painful was being raised solely by a classic, paranoid mother, whose reality did not match the world's reality. Painful was attending the funeral of my father who was a stranger to me. Painful was my miscarriage. Painful was my mother-in-law's suicide. Painful was my own mother's death. Painful was my divorce and L's hatred.

Nevertheless, the heart-breaking pain comes from losing a relationship with one born from your own body.

True Stories about Alcohol

I realize that you are adults who must make all your own decisions; nevertheless, I feel compelled to lay out the facts regarding alcohol for your consideration.

Alcohol is not your friend. It fuzzes your brain and impairs your judgment. Deep down you already know this to be truth.

My grandfather died in a car wreck at age 58 because of alcohol. He and his son had been drinking with the good ole boys. On the drive home, they ran into the back of a big truck. Had he never taken the first drink of alcohol, he would probably have lived to meet his other three grandchildren. Alcohol was not his friend.

My cousin's daughter died in a car wreck in 1991 at age 22 because of alcohol. If she had not accepted a ride with someone using alcohol, she would probably have lived a full life. Alcohol was not her friend.

My son-in-law died in a car wreck in March 2000 at age 37 because of alcohol. If he had never taken his first drink of alcohol, he would probably have lived a full life, and his daughter would not be missing out on having a father like the other kids. Alcohol was not his friend.

My mother-in-law died from a gun in her hand while "under the influence" of alcohol in 1978. If she had never taken her first drink, she could have watched her grandchildren grow up. Alcohol was not her friend.

My uncle lived most of his 76 years dependent on alcohol. The alcohol robbed him of financial gain, good family stability, and a feeling of personal self-worth. It also left scars on his son and daughter and his incredibly patient wife. If he never took his first drink, life would have been immeasurably better for all of them. Alcohol was not his friend.

My daughter's senior business partner lost his license to practice medicine because his body became dependent upon alcohol and prescription medication. If he had never taken his first drink, he would not have become addicted. Alcohol was not his friend.

People say that one's metabolism affects whether or not they will become alcohol dependent. The problem is that one's metabolism does not speak up and alert the individual during those first drinks that he or she will become an alcoholic. The person is unknowingly led down a path that can lead to a sad life, or an early death.

Some people justify the use of alcohol from the standpoint of "moderation in all things." From my viewpoint, that does not stand up. What about the recovering alcoholic who lives by the motto of "one day at a time without alcohol with God's help?" What if he (or she) indulged in just one "moderate" drink?

How is the alcoholic different from you? Only because we know <u>after the fact</u> that his metabolism was susceptible to alcohol. We don't know <u>ahead</u> of time about anyone's metabolism regarding alcohol addiction.

There, but for the grace of God, go I. I could be an alcoholic. I don't want to risk finding out. Life offers a smorgasbord of choices throughout life, many of which prove to be harmful to us.

Some people tend to play Russian roulette with alcohol. I will pray that none of you become addicted to alcohol. Here is the last thing I plan to ever say on the subject: ALCOHOL IS NOT YOUR FRIEND! The same is true for drugs!

Praise for Rex

After Rex's wife died in 1990, we became <u>best friends</u> from 1991–2013. We married in 2013 to keep Rex out of a nursing home. I became his main caregiver and he lived 13 more months to age 93.

Rex W. Rinker

All of the following are things for which I am thankful:
- that Rex has been part of my life since 1991 to 2014.
- that he has so often been my supportive shoulder and listening ear. He takes the time to truly listen.
- that he builds my morale with his quiet little sense of humor.
- that he finds the "lost" items in my home (such as my glasses), for which I have "thoroughly" searched.
- that he does a million little things that I cannot do such as opening jars, fixing radios, fixing clocks.
- that he opens the car doors for me no matter how windy or rainy the weather.
- that he collaborated with me on special projects such as the small patio

by the back door, and the white picket fence by the side of the house.
- that he assisted me and enabled me to do many things that I would not have been able to do without him.
- that he painstakingly worked on the walnut table, bringing it from a pile of old wood pieces to a lovely table.
- that he drove with me out-of-state to Aunt Willie's funeral, and gave me the support I needed when M lashed out at me.
- that he almost never complained of his ailments when I know he must have had at least a few.
- that he gave me a big massager (chiropractic type), which has been a real God-send.
- that he checked on me when I'm sick, goes to the grocery store during my illness, and even led me to the shower when I was too ill to walk alone.
- that after realizing how fond I am of my old wind-up watch, he made arrangements with a local jeweler to make it battery operated. Now I prefer it even over the new modern watch I received at retirement.
- that he altered my new "bird clock" so that the loud hourly bird sounds would be silent.
- that when I wanted a backup fuel for my kerosene heaters for Y2K, Rex took 50 gal. drums and created a faucet for each, then built a cradle whereby they could lie on their sides in my garage and could house the necessary kerosene fuel. The man is a genius.
- that when a member of my family would disappoint or hurt me thereby pulling me down, he would build me back up; he made me feel special
- that when a beautiful, intelligent stray cat came and adopted my home, Rex learned to love her just as I did. We accepted her independence and royal ways. When she was killed by some wild animal, Rex went to his workshop and lovingly built a proper box of his finest walnut wood to bury her in; then he buried her in my flower bed at the far back of the yard.

I have come to the conclusion that there is nothing that he can't do. Also, I think that he is my guardian angel that God provided for these last years. And I think he is as close to being a saint as anyone I know.

Rex had built his own movie theater which seated 22. He used it for church groups and clubs to see old movies with a sound projector.

Life at 518 East Moler Avenue

Within the first year in our "new" (one-hundred-year-old) house, M and I both began to notice unexplainable things occurring within the house. Lights off and on, radios off and on, a knock at the door, etc. It was no small thing to decide that we shared the house with a ghost. At first, we were petrified. On one occasion after "someone" shook the bed, we fled and sat in Hardee's from 5:00 am until time for school and work. Poor M at Hardee's trying to study for school exams.

I went to the courthouse to learn the history of the house. I learned that the previous family had been here for about 40 years, but the house had been owned by three other families also. The house was built in 1917. I had purchased it from a family who's blind son, Clifford, had died at about age 50 from a heart attack and then falling down the stairs a few years before we moved in. Naturally, we wondered if the ghost could be Clifford. We nicknamed the ghost Casper.

On occasion, we spent the night at the home of various friends when things got too intense. We stayed at B's, at C's near Gerrard town, at M's friend J's on High Street. My boss, brought over a preacher friend who went through the house trying to rid it of the ghost (unsuccessfully). He prayed throughout the house and placed little pieces of white cloth in various areas.

Another friend insisted that I tell her friend at a gathering about the details. He promised to come over and see what he could do, but he never called or came. (I think he probably used the material for a book he was writing.) Another friend S, wanted to go with me to the attic to search for answers. We haltingly did so, but turned up nothing that answered the ghost dilemma.

We were not the only observers of the "activity." Once when unsuspecting friends of M's were here, the kitchen dishes started "rattling" in the dish drain. When C and D chose to spend the night here to observe, D, who went to bed ahead of us, heard footsteps and music. C received a "scratch" upon her face from an invisible hand.

One day V and I together heard a "cat" meowing from under the desk in the dining room. (Our cat, Sherb, was outside the house at the time.) One of the most dramatic for me was when the lid of a pill bottle I had sitting on the kitchen counter was thrown <u>across the room</u> and hit the side of the refrigerator.

Not surprisingly, my blood pressure and menstrual periods were both bouncing around like crazy. I was steadily getting reactions to my allergy shots, such as stinging pain and nerve jumping in my leg, or leg numbness, or isolated pain in my head. I suspected the glycerin in the shots was the problem, since my previous shots with Dr. L had used saline rather than glycerin. (Somehow, I managed an evening speech class at Shepherd as an extension from WVU at master's level.) Dr. M recommended a partial hysterectomy, removing the uterus, which was accomplished on 10/30/85, a day after my 49th birthday.

<u>On the night before the surgery</u>, just before I went to sleep, into my room drifted the head of an apparition. It came closer and closer to me. Just at my face, it whispered, "there are things that we didn't know." With my reaction of jerking fear, it disappeared just as I realized that it was my mother. Mom had passed away about 1½ years earlier, and always had a habit of getting right down to your ear to tell you a secret! Would she have told me anything further if I had not reacted with such fear? No way to know.

I went into the surgery calmly, except that I was afraid of what I might say while under anesthesia—such as about my infidelity. At that point, such was my main concern rather than the surgery. I figured, get the surgery, and get on with life. I had even casually told M to go on to her class at Shepherd, since my friend had said she would visit that afternoon. (BAD MISTAKE.)

When I was back in my room I had catheters going all directions, and I was so cold my teeth were chattering. Problem was, the call button on my bed was located <u>beyond my reach</u>. So, I had no choice but to wait until someone showed up who could cover me to make me warmer. S never came; no nursing personnel ever came to my room until the shift changed at 3:00 pm. Alive, but 100% miserable describes me. Finally, a compassionate nurse showed up and helped me get pajamas and a blanket, bless her heart. The next day, I learned that Dr. M had cut my bladder in the process of removing the uterus through the vagina, so I had stayed twice as long in surgery, and I would have to take home with me the super pubic catheter now inserted through my skin and into my bladder.

A week later I had to return to the doctor's office to have the catheter removed from the bladder. M (then 17) drove me over to Winchester to the doctor's office. I will never forget that ride. I felt extremely fragile with that catheter hanging out of my body, and my 17-year-old daughter driving the speed limit and above in spite of my requests to slow down. I cried most of the way there. There was no car wreck, but I felt like an emotional wreck when we arrived in Winchester, VA.

My allergy shots were not going well; my blood pressure bounced around, and my bladder was leaking when I sneezed. I was noticing a slight numbness in my right leg, presumably from the shot. Often, I had black and blue places on my arms and legs from hitting a small capillary. M (age 17) continued to display her temper tantrums and sometimes came home at 2:00 am or 3:00 am as we drifted into 1986. I managed to sandwich in Thursday night choir practice, various doctor's appointments, singing weekly at the VA Chapel, M asked MB over for supper occasionally, but she was dating several people.

During February, I had a twitch or quiver in my left foot for ten days, Dr. B froze a wart off my hand, I was home with sinus infection for about eight days, and on one of those days Casper (ghost) shook my bed! Was it any wonder that my blood pressure became unstable?

April of 1986 was a very active month for the ghost, Casper. Even though my boss, J, and his preacher friend had prayed over the house at the first of the month, activity was noticed throughout the month more than ever before. C and D spent the night there with us, and some nights we stayed at the home of friends. One morning as we awakened, we found a picture (small and old) of my mother's cousin, Virginia, on the foot of M's bed. The picture had previously been in my Mom's very old picture album now located here at my house. How did it get on the bed, and why?? From about April 12 to April 28, there was "activity" every night. You may wonder how I know all these dates. I have kept a small "Hallmark datebook" every year since 1980

Ponderings

or before. In that datebook, I list appointments, and other significant events. And those "happenings" certainly seemed significant enough to write down in my datebook.

During the next few years, we noted that each April seemed to be the heaviest month of "activity." My mother had died in April; I wondered what month Clifford died. A former neighbor said it was sometime in the spring.

M continued her pattern of temper tantrums, but she slept in my bed fairly often because of her fright over the ghost. M graduated June 1, 1986 with several honors. She received several small scholarships; enough to pay for her first year at Shepherd College and part of the second year. M took two courses during the summer and thereby got a head start on the year; in fact, she took heavy hours every semester and thereby graduated in three years. Since I had pushed myself and completed college in three years, I was not recommending it; but I think she did it partly to show me that she could do it too!

A Meltdown

On February 26, 2013 about 3:00 am I had a "meltdown" of tears and prayers to God while only my senior cat and God watched.

Two things converged—my inability to change the dangerous behavior of my 14-year-old Callie, nor the dangerous behavior of my 92-year-old friend, Rex.

On 12/2/12 I began care-giver duties for my friend Rex, fixing two meals a day for us at his home (without pay) usually 11:00 am–6:00 pm, seven days per week. My duties included buying all the groceries, etc. After almost three months without a break except one day when I was sick in bed, and one day of sleet, I was mentally and physically exhausted. No one from inside the church nor outside the church stepped forward to offer to carry one day per week.

Rex had a major heart attack over three years before leaving him with a major blood clot and aneurysm in his heart. Two years ago, following a tooth hurting, a dentist told him he had seven teeth which needed removal by surgery. When Rex refused the surgery, I suggested he use hydrogen peroxide two times a day to heal the infections. Amazingly, Rex never complained again about his teeth until about January 26, 2013. I figured hydrogen peroxide might be the answer again, so I suggested the early morning care giver have Rex routinely use it after breakfast.

Ponderings

After a couple of weeks, Rex began to feel better and have more energy. He even shopped in Walmart with his own cart and lifted a 12 pack of cokes! His health seemed better than before Nov. 27!

On Feb. 26, he refused to use the hydrogen peroxide saying his mouth felt fine. My talk to him only made him angry. He did not want to be "bossed." He said he had used the hydrogen peroxide for a sore throat. He had <u>totally forgotten</u> his toothache from weeks before. How could I change his behavior (in order to help him)??

Now to Callie cat. Weeks ago, she started to pull up the heat vent near my bed. Once she learned that she could do that, there was no stopping her! Before Nov. 27, Rex would have come over to my house and permanently made the vent stationary. He would have solved the problem. Now, I tried scolding Callie, and frequently waking up during the night to place the heat vent back over the hole in the floor. One morning, I discovered that Callie had dragged two live electric cords down into the hole (of heat vent). I moved the radio, and its cord across the room, and turned the electric heater around, but I knew I had to find a better solution.

I put duct tape around the heat vent and wondered whether the heat would make the tape less strong. Callie laid against the vent for heat and, at first, seemed to accept the duct tape. Then I would hear Callie pulling at the tape during the night, so I would awaken and yell at her to stop!

On Feb. 26, 2013, the same night of Rex's refusal of the hydrogen peroxide, Callie woke me with her attempts to pull up the vent! I was itching with hives/eczema/allergies! I switched on the bed side light and smacked her once with my hand as I yelled at her to stop it! I felt remorse for hitting her and she just looked at me.

When she tried pulling at the tape again, I hit her once with the wooden spoon in my hand assuming I would hit fat, but I hit bone! She seemed fine, but I went into a meltdown of tears and prayers! Callie sympathetically watched me crying and praying about both the cat and my friend Rex. I begged God for an answer as to how to handle both problems.

To my mind came the idea of putting a smell in the vent which would deter her...campho-phenique from my bedside table! She took one sniff and walked away. I said, "thank you, Lord."

Looking at Religion

One subject I have not yet tackled is that of religion. With friends, I generally never discuss religion and politics. However, in this all-inclusive autobiography, I choose to include my view on God, Christ, religion, and preachers.

First, I want to talk about preachers. In my 65 years, I have known such a variety, many of who "fell from grace" either publicly or privately. Rev. W stole money from my mother and many other faithful viewers to subsidize his lavish lifestyle. Even worse was the leader of the PTL Club, Jim Baker, and his wife Tammie Faye. Baker spent some time in prison, but I hear that he is getting back in the preaching business, and I guess some people will follow him again.

I have known of homosexual preachers and church organists. The brother of my friend, C, was a Lutheran minister at a church in New York for many years, and was also a practicing homosexual. I assume that his parishioners did not know of his private lifestyle. C now tells me that he lives in Florida, works for hospice, and has a male life-partner.

When I worked at the IRS, I gradually became aware of a black man there who played the organ for his church and was gay. When a little choir was formed at IRS-MCC, he was chosen to direct us. Once I went to his apartment to practice for a program; while there, I met a white school teacher that my instincts

Ponderings

told me was his "partner." After we practiced the song, I stayed on and sang some songs since D played beautifully. I am sure the phone call was the partner asking if I had left. When I went to my car, I found that my radio antenna had been bent double and broke off in my hand. I guess my visit had lasted too long. I never replaced it, since I seldom listened to the radio.

The lid came off the perversion existing within the Catholic church, and it hit television and magazines. Apparently, many children have been scarred for life by the very people who were trusted to guide them toward God.

In Lee town, WV at the little Baptist Church where C and K H attended, a relationship developed between the preacher and the organist. They both left their spouses and families, and moved to another state.

B B and her husband D chose to attend an active, non-denominational church in Hagerstown, MD; in fact, they were married in that church, and I was her matron-of-honor. I heard B often speak of trips the pastor took such as to Africa.

Around early 2001, B mentioned that the pastor gave up the pulpit to his wife. He was selling cars in Hagerstown, and did not even attend the service Hum-m-m. B did not appear to think this was unusual. Then about a year later, she told me that the church no longer existed. Everyone scattered to other churches. My mind wonders how much money the pastor and his wife took with them from the church. When the building is sold, who gets the money??

When M and J moved to Mt. Airy, they became acquainted with her pregnant patient who was the wife of a local Lutheran minister, and the woman was also a certified minister. M and J started to attend their church, and the two couples became really good friends. In fact, that minister christened H in a service before J died. We have pictures.

Shortly thereafter, they (C and C) moved to Greensboro where they were able to pastor separate churches. M still visits their home occasionally. I attended one service with M in Christine's church where she is assistant pastor in Greensboro. She is a congenial, upbeat person. So, you ask, what's the point. Shortly after I moved here, I learned from M that both ministers are practicing members of a nudist colony. They now have a second child, and I wonder if they are still pursuing the nudist lifestyle.

All this is leading me to say one thing. It is imperative that we keep our eyes on God and not on <u>any</u> preacher because he may be unable to resist the world's temptations any better than others in or out of the church.

I believe that God sent Christ as a means of our existing into eternity in heaven after we complete our life here on earth (if we believe in Him). I align myself with the protestant religion, but no particular denomination, even though I have been both Baptist and Methodist.

I have no idea what god will do about those people who have never had a chance to hear about Jesus. But, I find that there are many other things to which we will not get answers while we live here on earth, and that's okay. When I was younger, it was definitely not okay; I thought I had to have answers to my questions.

People argue about whether it is "once saved, always saved," or whether a fall from grace can put one in a position to miss heaven. I don't have the answer, but I hope to keep in daily contact with God, so that I can ask him for forgiveness for my most recent, foolish sins.

I believe that nearly all lawyers and many preachers will have more on their list to account to God for at their passing than most other folks because they were in a position to lead or mislead other souls. That is more than my personal observation; there is bible scripture to back up this comment.

My evening prayer usually begins by asking God's blessings on family and friends followed by the request for wisdom, insight, knowledge, understanding, discernment, faith, and love for each of us. I then ask for our guardian angels to watch over us, then for help to seek after righteousness, sidestep temptations and pitfalls, and seek to do God's will. Next, I ask God to fill each of us with his holy spirit and holy love. Next, I ask Him to help us be cautious about our mind/thoughts, eyes, nose, mouth, ears, heart, and will; that we will keep them all stayed on Him and thereby resist temptations. Lastly, I ask Him to let us each do something to please Him. This has been a culmination of things I have learned along the way.

Adopted by a Cat

I had moved to Mt. Airy NC in year 2000 to help my daughter with her two-year-old daughter. My back yard required a great deal of landscaping and flower planting including azalea bushes.

As I worked out back each day, I noticed an almost-grown calico cat watching me. Everywhere I went, she went too. From the start, she adopted me!

Eventually, I learned that she had lived around the corner with two other outdoor cats; but she never left me. I named her Callie, then learned that Callie was already her name! When fall/winter came, I moved her inside and offered a litter box. She refused the box and went to the door to be allowed outside for the bathroom, even at four in the morning. When she touched my curtain in my bedroom, that was her signal to get up and open the door. When she wanted back inside at night she touched my bedroom window! Smart cookie! This all was wonderful for me because I am allergic to both cats and a litter box!

Seven years later when Callie and I moved to Martinsburg, WV to the house at Silver Lane, everything changed. As she made her first trip to the back porch, dogs barked at her from each side and behind! She was so traumatized she never went outside again for six months! Thus, began the dreaded litter box, which was hard on my allergies. When she thought I devoted too much time to the computer, she climbed into the dish drainer for attention. What personality she had!

When I became the main caregiver for Rex she had too much alone time and was very lonely. When Rex and I married to keep him out of the nursing home, Callie and I moved over to his house and left my home sitting unoccupied.

Callie developed a tumor behind her left eye, which made her behave out-of-her-head about once every ten days, for maybe two hours before she slept, exhausted. During those episodes, she would entangle herself under Rex's hospice bed and was very hard to rescue.

One year after Rex passed away, Callie and I moved to Greeneville, Tennessee. Amazingly, her tumor and episodes disappeared, but her health was fragile because she was 17. That dear soul died ten months after we came to TN. She enriched my life so very much. She is in a crematory box waiting for me. We will be buried together at a family cemetery near Selma, NC.

A Trip to the Cemetery

 Within Rex's last couple of years of life, he wanted to be sure that a childhood friend had a tombstone, so one day we went walking through tall grass at one of the oldest cemeteries in Martinsburg, WV, called Green Hill Cemetery.

 Eventually we were joined by the caretaker, a woman about age 50-55 who tried to assist us. Rex was almost sure the grave was in a certain area, but couldn't find his name. After a lot of searching the caretaker led us to find him buried next to his mother and his own tombstone. That knowledge pleased Rex.

 The caregiver told me that I had an "interesting energy." I sort of hid behind Rex verbally saying, "Oh, I'm just helping him find someone." I wondered what she meant, but I did not ask.

The End

JESUS LOVES ME,

JUST AS I AM,

PRAISE BE TO GOD.

About the Author

Myra "Gail" Carpenter is a senior who is publishing her first book at age 80. Her career has included school teacher, employment counselor, and secretary. She has two adult children and nine grandchildren. Three loving cats have shared her life at different stages, and they have enriched her days.

www.ingramcontent.com/pod-product-compliance
Lightning Source LLC
Chambersburg PA
CBHW022109040426
42451CB00007B/191